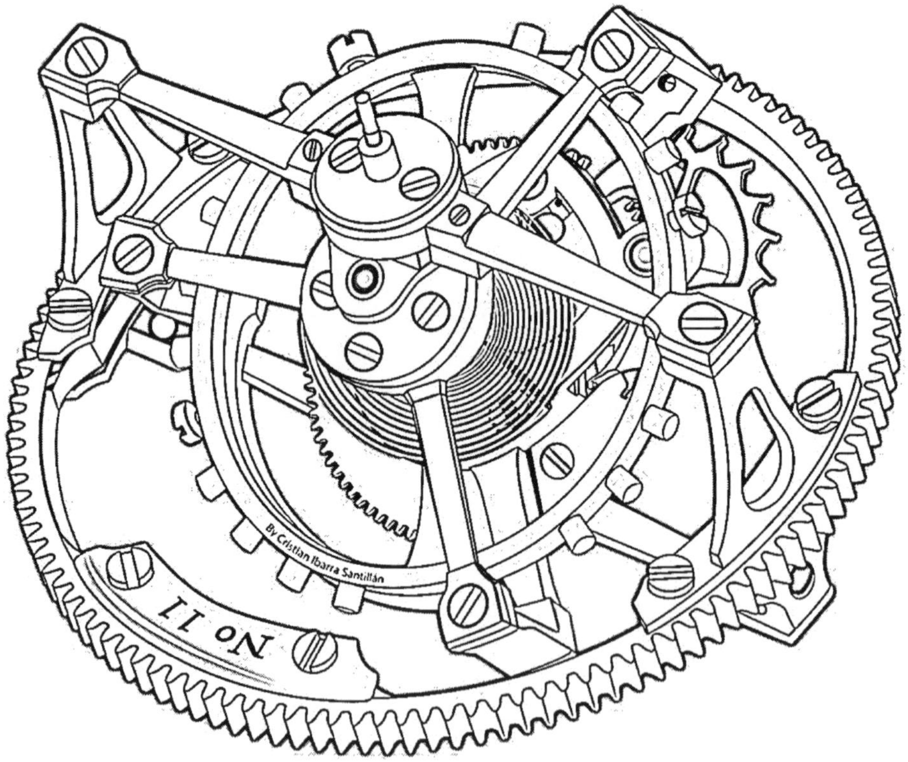
By Cristian Ibarra Santillán
No 11

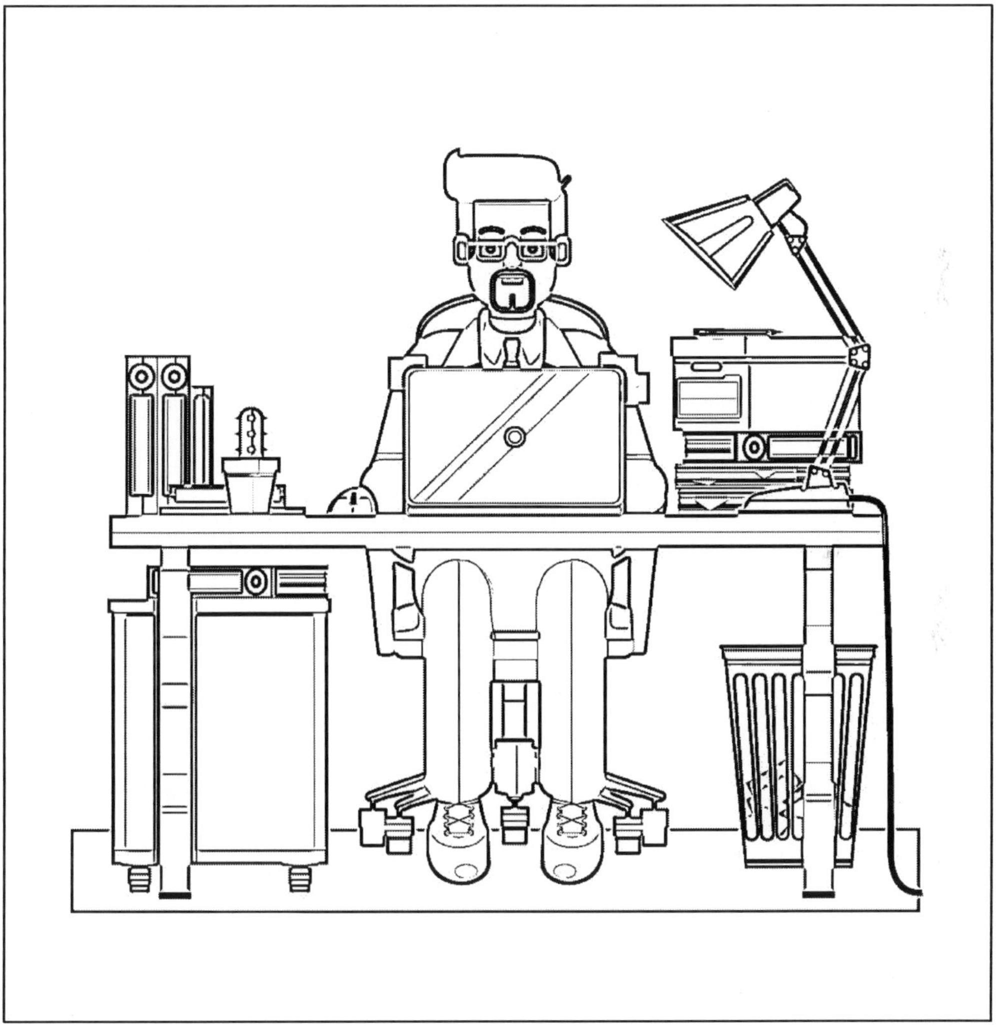

YOU
LIKE!
SMOKE!
I LIKE!

CAFE
CAFE
CAFE
CAFE
CAFE
CAFE

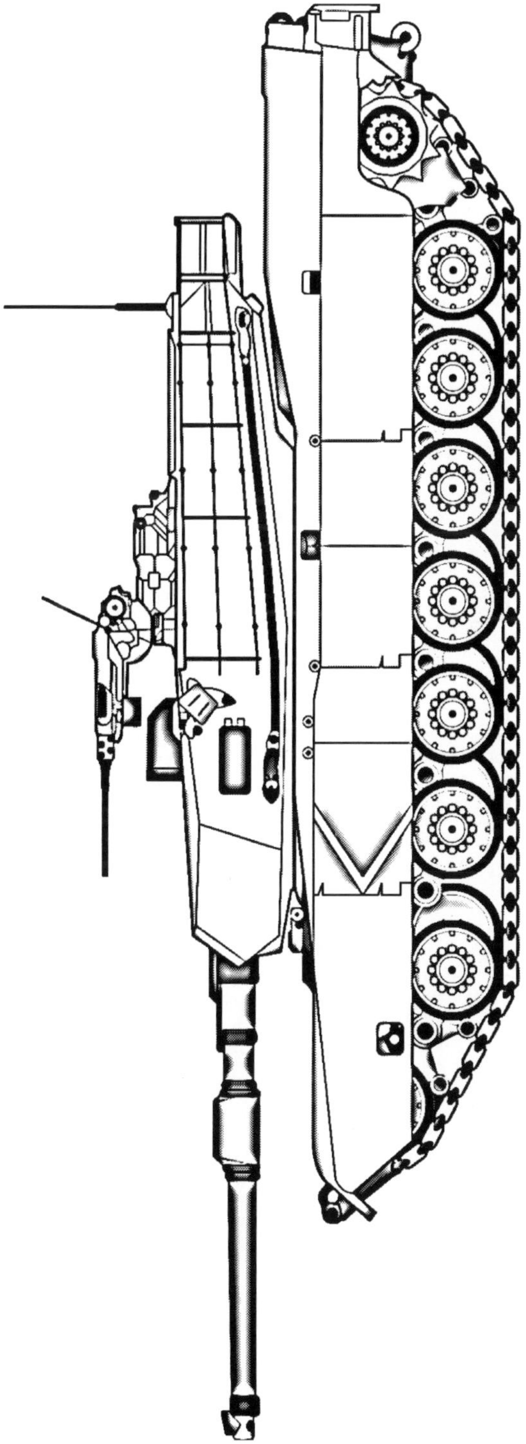

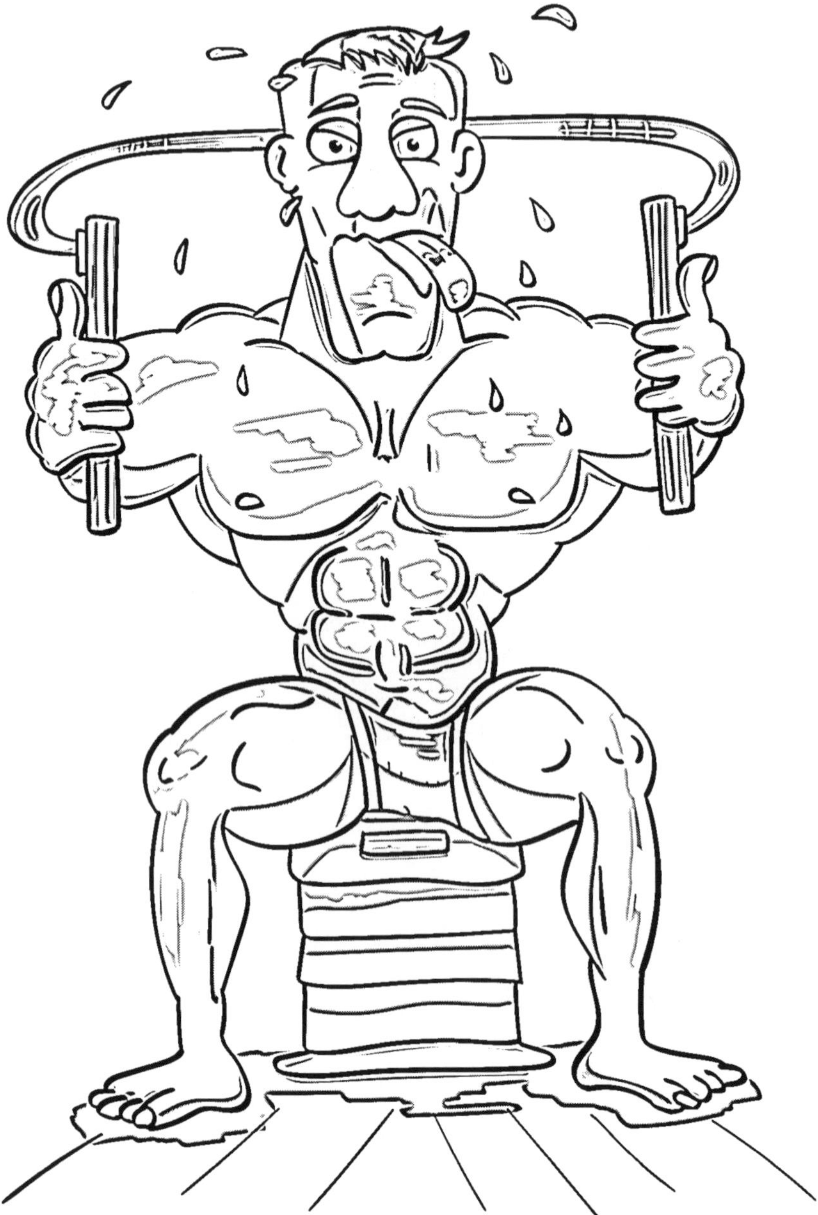

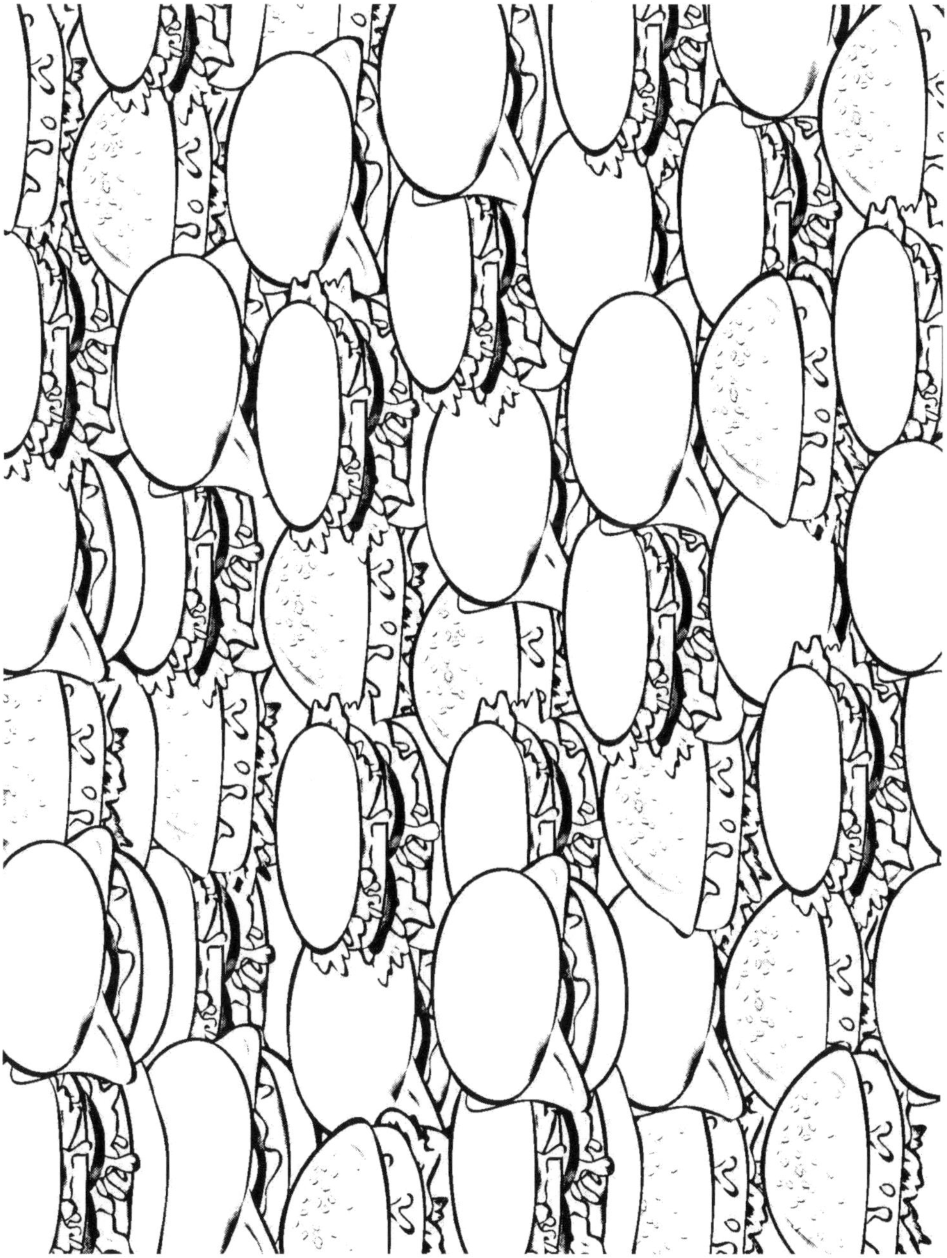

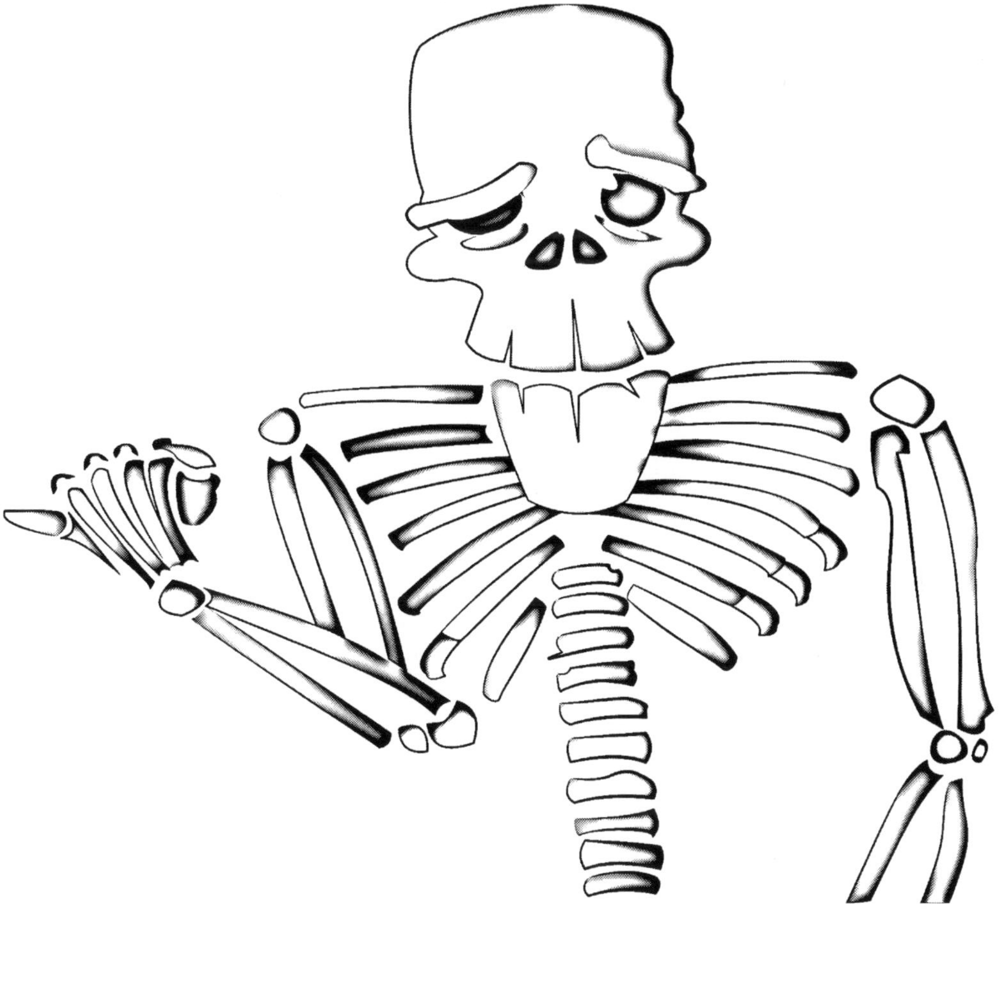

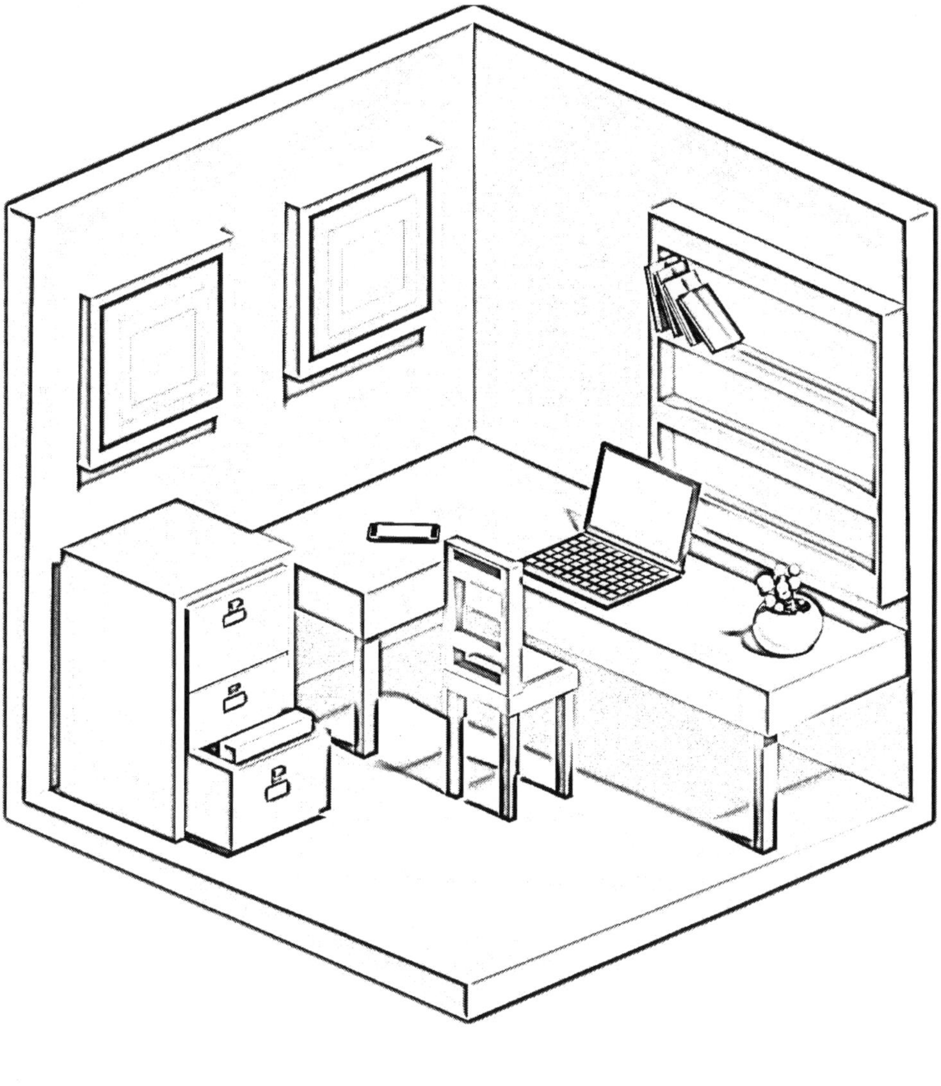

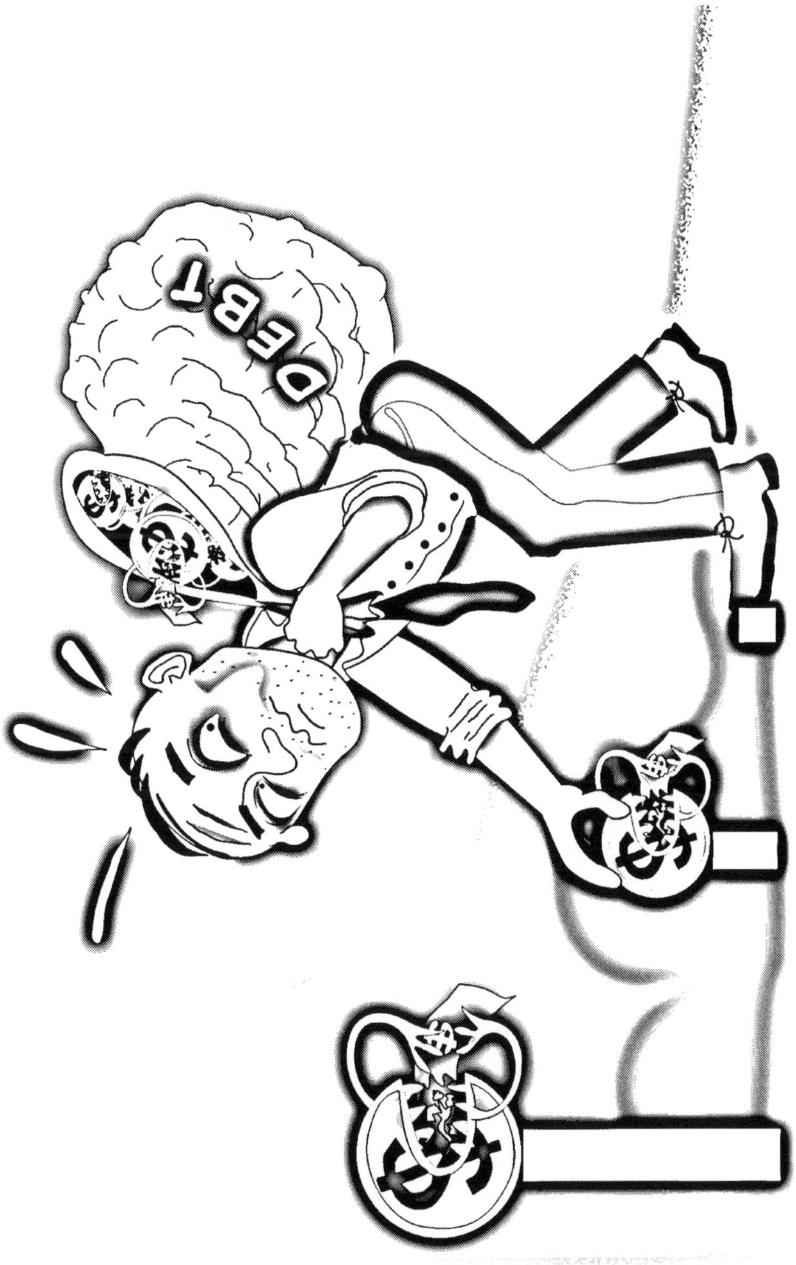
DEBT

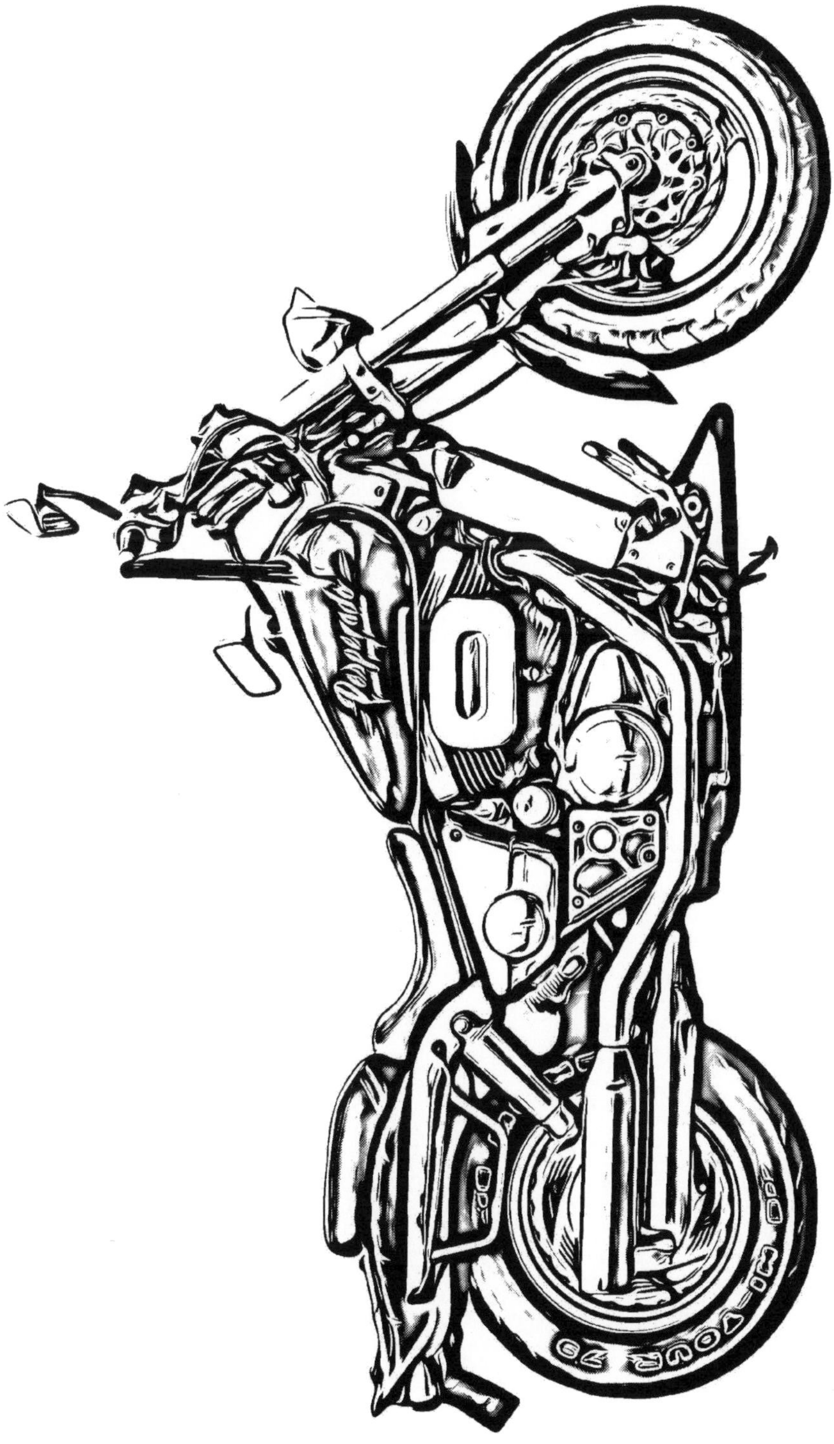

7

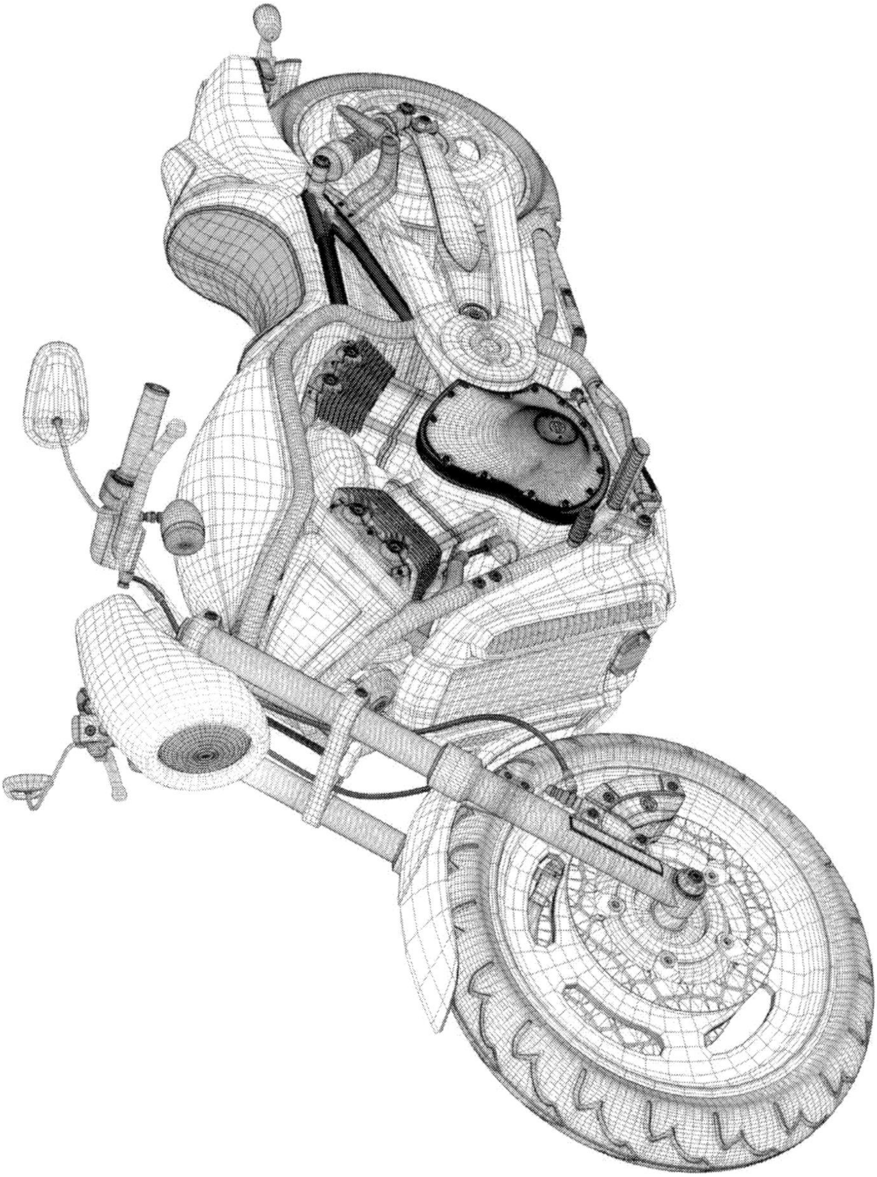

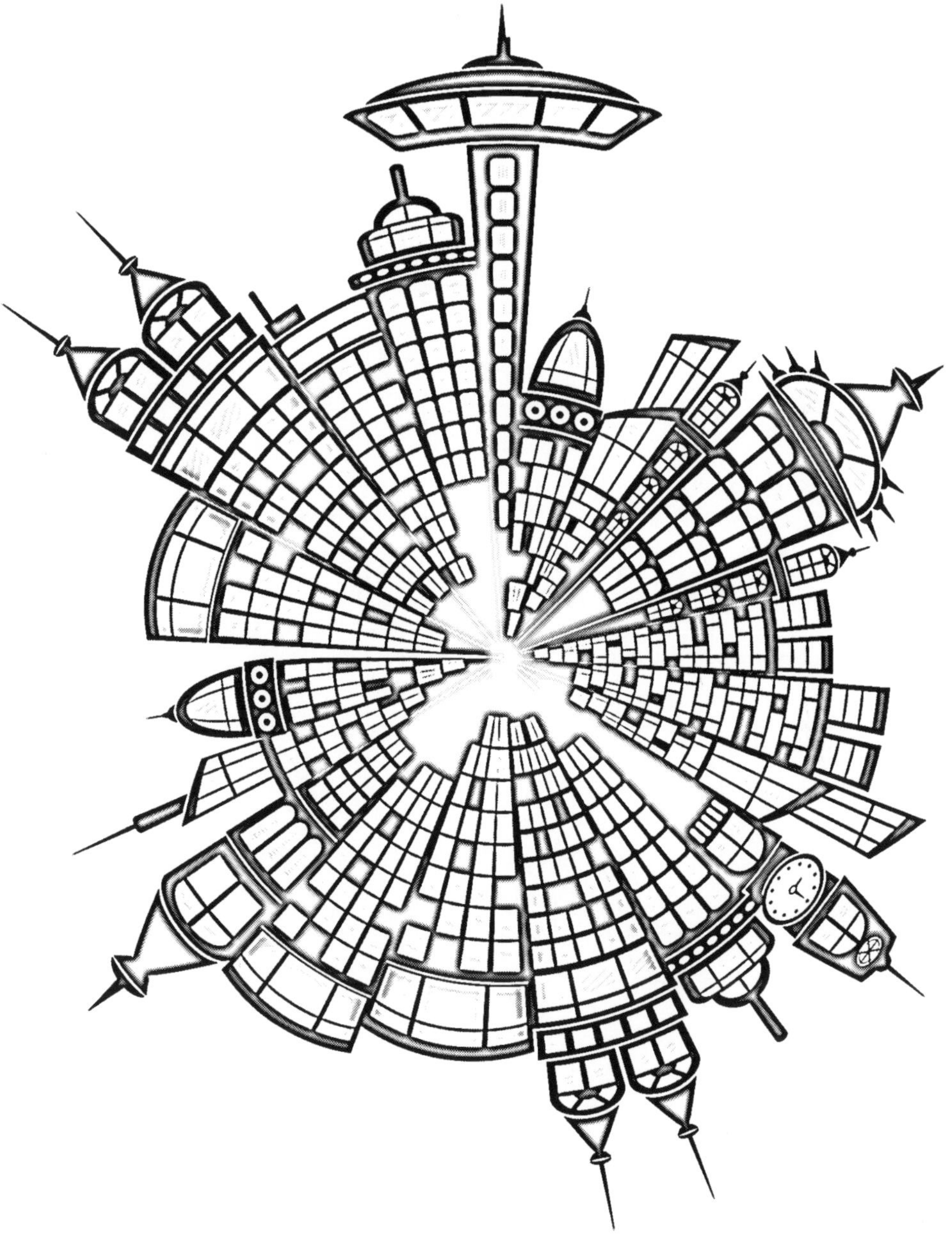

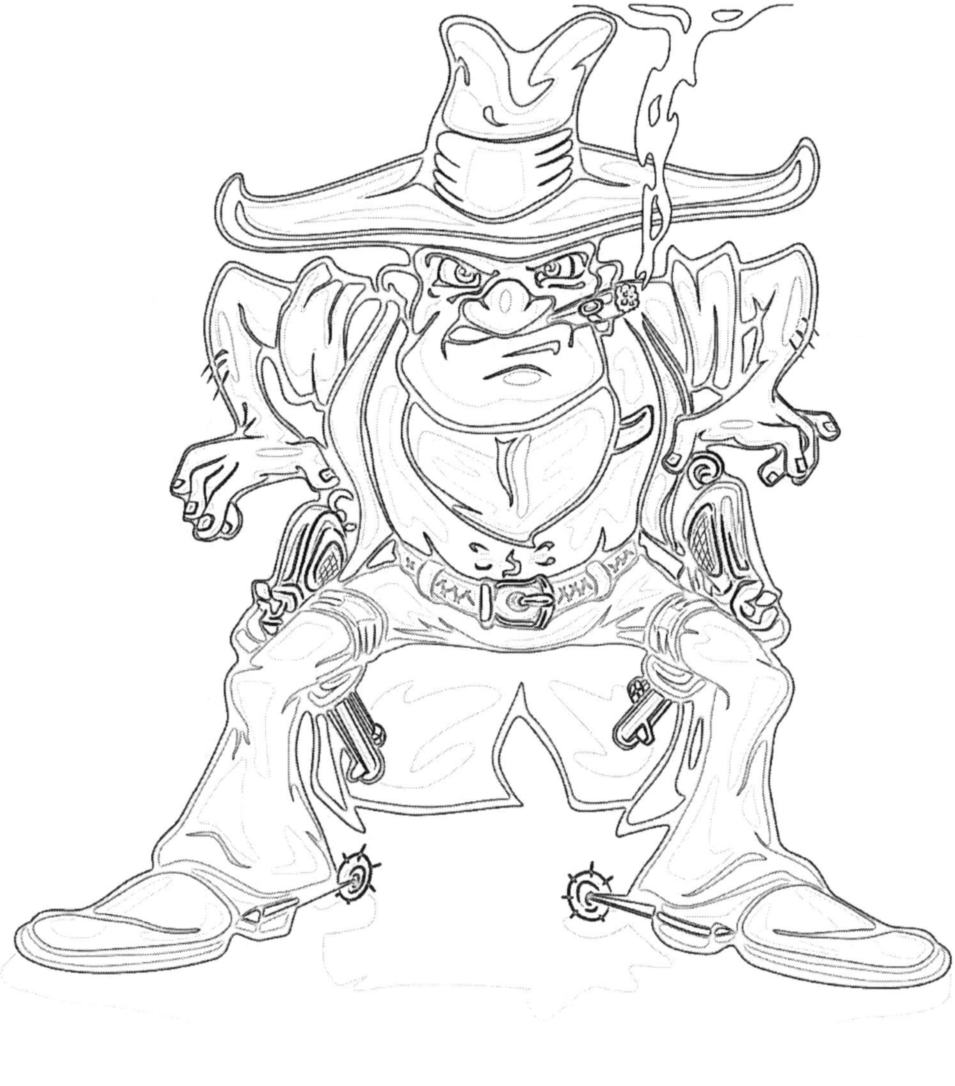

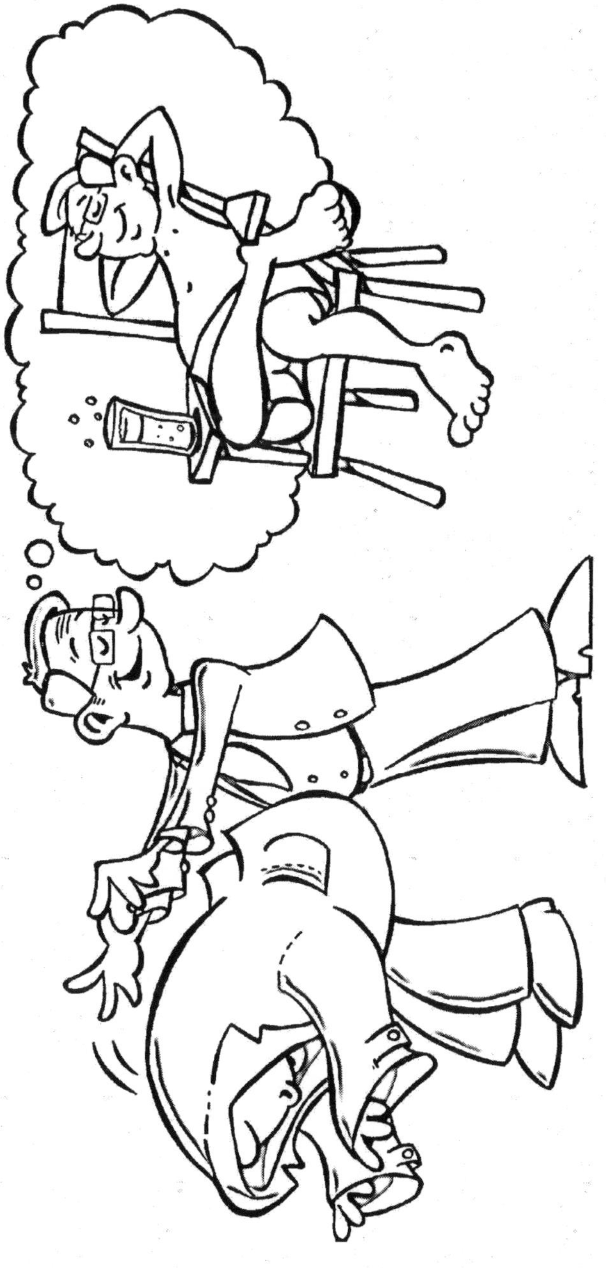

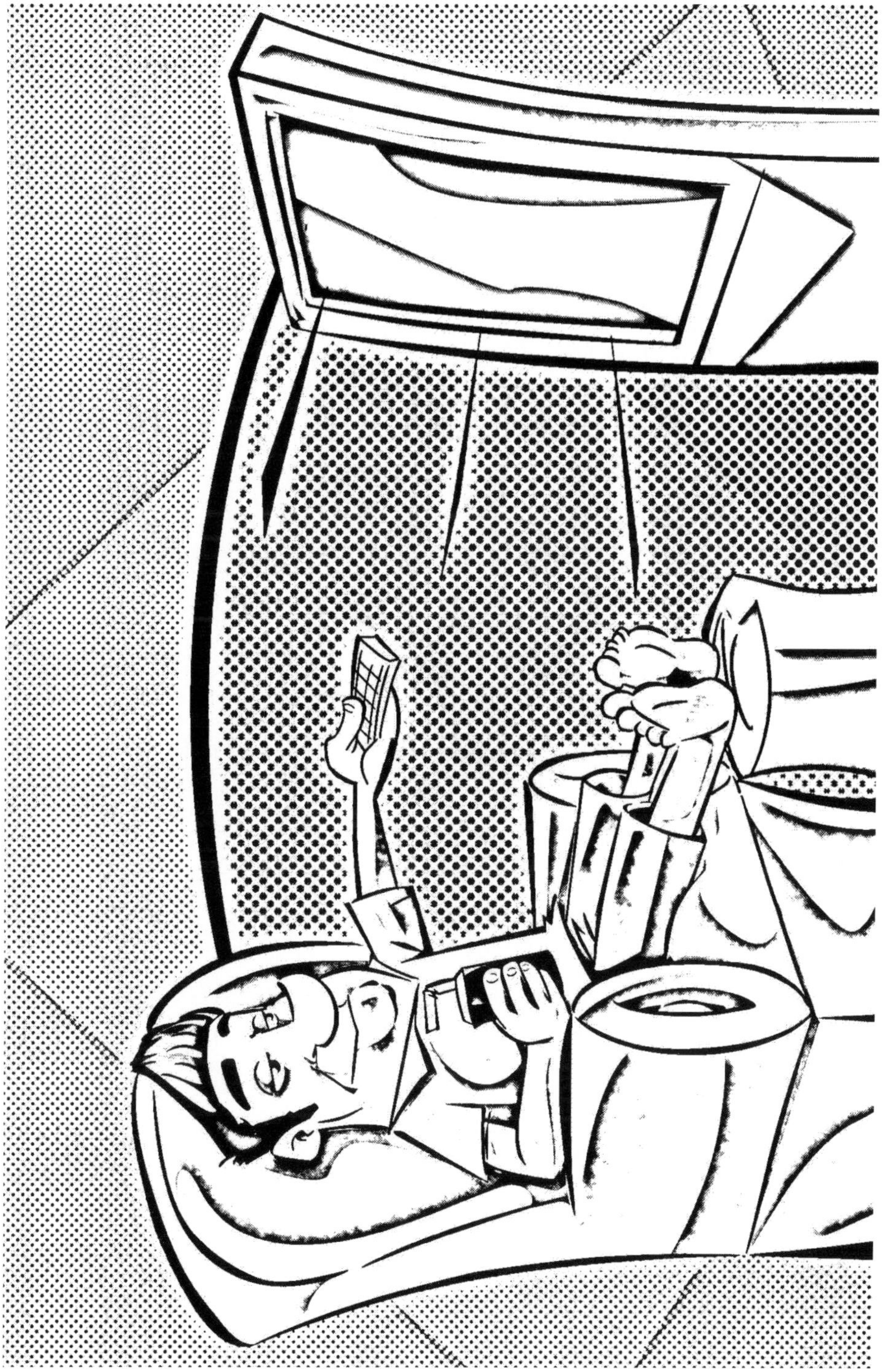

Under Construction

Printed in Great
Britain
by Amazon

31568172R00054